MW01171948

Coloring sections purchased from adobe photostock

Foreword

For many years I was stuck in the rat-race we call "corporate world" I was stressed out, exhausted. I became sick, depression was looming over me, I gained a lot of weight and overall I was powered out and unhappy.

When I decided to change my life around and become a Licensed Massage Therapist, I not only changed my on life, I started to help my clients to change their lives as well.

As a practicing, Licensed Massage Therapist, I see every day during my work, how detrimental stress is and the damage it can do to our physical bodies.

Stress can manifest itself in tight, sore muscles, unexplained pain in areas of the body we would never suspect to look for stress points.

Our lives today are fast paced, demanding, filled with deadlines, chores, obligations, demands, worries of money, health, careers, family.

It is "normal" to power up as well as recharge all sorts of gadgets and daily electronic aids to help us in our daily lives. But rarely do we stop and consider that we need to recharge our own batteries as well.

If we forget to recharge our cell phone, it stops to function. The same rings true for our bodies, mind and soul.

I created this journal to help you relax, rest, find the positive things in your life and ultimately recharge your batteries.

AND:

If you do find yourself with more time on your hand, contact a trusted licensed or certified massage therapist in your area and schedule an appointment for a therapeutic and relaxing massage.

How to use this journal

This journal has 52 pages for 52 weeks in the calendar year.

Recharging your batteries does not need to take up a lot of time or lengthy commitments. If we would have a lot of free time on our hands, we would not be stressed and burnt out!

Once a week, open up this journal and use 1 page a week to help you recharge and relax. If you need to, make an appointment with yourself in your appointment book or calendar, carve out 20 minutes a week to heal yourself.

The corner picture is for coloring. Most of us enjoyed coloring books when we were little, we forgot everything around us and filled our mind with ideas how our coloring page would look like when we were finished. Grab some markers, coloring pencils, water colors, whatever you feel like. Start coloring, These areas are small enough to not take up too much time but they will help you leave your stressful day behind for a couple of minutes.

The lines on the page are there to help you surround yourself with positivity. It is easy to surround ourselves with negative words all day long. The commute to work was filled with traffic jams, the deadline is looming, the kids have the sniffles. Negativity attracts negativity. Negativity creates stress.

Surround yourself with positive thoughts instead. Find something positive that you experienced this week and write it down. It can be big, it can be mundane. Maybe you saw a beautiful sunset. Maybe a pretty flower on the side of the road. Maybe you only missed 1 dead line this week and not 2. Maybe your child had 1 asthma attach and not 3.

The last part of the page is a small exercise for you to do. Again, they will only take up a couple of minutes of your busy day but they will help you de-stress and recharge.

And remember, you scheduled 20-30 minutes of the week to do the journal page!

Example week

This week I am thankful for:
_____
_____

_____

Maybe you saw a beautiful sunset?

A pretty flower on the side of the

 road?

I only had 1 asthma attack a day and not 4.

It can be something important or mundane. But

it should be positive.

If we surround our self with positive thoughts, we

become more positive our self over time.

_____

_____

_____

_____

_____

_____

2 Minute Candle Meditation

Light a tea candle and set it in a safe place. Set a timer for 2 minutes.
Sit in front of the candle and look into the flame. Think only of the flame. Every
time your mind wanders, return back to the flame and continue to look at it.
Over time you will be able to look at the flame without your mind wandering. It
takes time. Start with short intervals.

Week 1

This week I am thankful for:

_____

_____

_____

_____

_____

_____

_____

_____

_____

_____

_____

_____

_____

_____

_____

_____

2 Minute Candle Meditation

Light a tea candle and set it in a safe place. Set a timer for 2 minutes.
Sit in front of the candle and look into the flame. Think only of the flame.
Every time your mind wanders, return back to the flame and continue to look
at it. Over time you will be able to look at the flame without your mind
wandering. It takes time. Start with short intervals

Week 2

This week I am thankful for:

_____

_____

_____

_____

_____

_____

_____

_____

_____

_____

_____

_____

_____

_____

_____

_____

2 Minute Zen Meditation

Seat yourself in a straight backed chair or sit on the floor with your back straight. Set a timer for 2 minutes.

Breath through your nose and keep your eyes lowered, resting your gaze on the ground about two to three feet in front of you.

Concentrate your attention on the movement of your breath going in and out through your nose. Each time you inhale, you count one number, starting with 10, and then moving backward to 9,8 etc. If you get distracted and lose your count, gently bring back the attention to 10 and resume from there.

Week 3

This week I am thankful for:

_____
_____
_____
_____
_____
_____
_____
_____
_____
_____
_____
_____
_____
_____
_____
_____
_____

2 Minute Loving Kindness Meditation

Set a timer for 2 minutes.
Sit in your meditation position, with closed eyes, and generate a feeling of kindness and benevolence in your heart and mind. Start by developing loving-kindness towards yourself.

Week 4

This week I am thankful for:

_____

_____

_____

_____

_____

_____

_____

_____

_____

_____

_____

_____

_____

_____

_____

_____

2 Minute Mantra Meditation

A mantra is a word or syllable without any particular meaning, that is repeated for the purpose of focusing the mind. It is not an affirmation. You can use any world you like. Some popular mantras are: Om, rama, yam, om namah padme hum. You can use any world you like. Whatever comes to your mind.

Seat yourself in a straight backed chair or sit on the floor with your back straight. Set a timer for 2 minutes.

Breath through your nose and keep your eyes closed. Repeat the mantra you chose in your mind over and over. Think of nothing but your mantra.

Week 5

This week I am thankful for:

_____

_____

_____

_____

_____

_____

_____

_____

_____

_____

_____

_____

_____

_____

_____

_____

2 Minute Third Eye Meditation

Set a timer for 2 minutes.

Sit in your meditation position and focus your attention on the "spot between the eyebrows" (this is sometimes called the "third eye"). If your mind wanders, redirect your thoughts back to this spot.

Week 6

This week I am thankful for:

_____

_____

_____

_____

_____

_____

_____

_____

_____

_____

_____

_____

_____

_____

_____

2 Minute Candle Meditation

Light a tea candle and set it in a safe place. Set a timer for 2 minutes.
Sit in front of the candle and look into the flame. Think only of the flame. Every time your mind wanders, return back to the flame and continue to look at it. Over time you will be able to look at the flame without your mind wandering. It takes time. Start with short intervals

Week 7

This week I am thankful for:

_____

_____

_____

_____

_____

_____

_____

_____

_____

_____

_____

_____

_____

_____

_____

_____

2 Minute Zen Meditation

Seat yourself in a straight backed chair or sit on the floor with your back straight. Set a timer for 2 minutes.

Breath through your nose and keep your eyes lowered, resting your gaze on the ground about two to three feet in front of you.

Concentrate your attention on the movement of your breath going in and out through your nose. Each time you inhale, you count one number, starting with 10, and then moving backward to 9,8 etc. If you get distracted and lose your count, gently bring back the attention to 10 and resume from there.

Week 8

This week I am thankful for:

_____

_____

_____

_____

_____

_____

_____

_____

_____

_____

_____

_____

_____

_____

_____

2 Minute Loving Kindness Meditation

Set a timer for 2 minutes.
Sit in your meditation position, with closed eyes, and generate a feeling of kindness and benevolence in your heart and mind. Start by developing loving-kindness towards yourself.

Week 9

This week I am thankful for:

_____

_____

_____

_____

_____

_____

_____

_____

_____

_____

_____

_____

_____

_____

_____

_____

2 Minute Mantra Meditation

A mantra is a word or syllable without any particular meaning, that is repeated for the purpose of focusing the mind. It is not an affirmation. You can use any world you like. Some popular mantras are: Om, rama, yam, om namah padme hum. You can use any world you like. Whatever comes to your mind.

Seat yourself in a straight backed chair or sit on the floor with your back straight. Set a timer for 2 minutes.

Breath through your nose and keep your eyes closed. Repeat the mantra you chose in your mind over and over. Think of nothing but your mantra.

Week 10

This week I am thankful for:

_____

_____

_____

_____

_____

_____

_____

_____

_____

_____

_____

_____

_____

_____

_____

_____

_____

2 Minute Third Eye Meditation

Set a timer for 2 minutes.

Sit in your meditation position and focus your attention on the "spot between the eyebrows" (this is sometimes called the "third eye"). If your mind wanders, redirect your thoughts back to this spot.

Week 11

This week I am thankful for:

_____

_____

_____

_____

_____

_____

_____

_____

_____

_____

_____

_____

_____

_____

_____

2 minute candle meditation

Light a tea candle and set it in a safe place. Set a timer for 2 minutes.
Sit in front of the candle and look into the flame. Think only of the flame. Every time your mind wanders, return back to the flame and continue to look at it. Over time you will be able to look at the flame without your mind wandering. It takes time. Start with short intervals

Week 12

This week I am thankful for:

_____

_____

_____

_____

_____

_____

_____

_____

_____

_____

_____

_____

_____

_____

_____

_____

2 Minute Zen Meditation

Seat yourself in a straight backed chair or sit on the floor with your back straight. Set a timer for 2 minutes.

Breath through your nose and keep your eyes lowered, resting your gaze on the ground about two to three feet in front of you.

Concentrate your attention on the movement of your breath going in and out through your nose. Each time you inhale, you count one number, starting with 10, and then moving backward to 9,8 etc. If you get distracted and lose your count, gently bring back the attention to 10 and resume from there.

Week 13

This week I am thankful for:

_____

_____

_____

_____

_____

_____

_____

_____

_____

_____

_____

_____

_____

_____

_____

_____

2 Minute Loving Kindness Meditation

Set a timer for 2 minutes.
Sit in your meditation position, with closed eyes, and generate a feeling of
kindness and benevolence in your heart and mind. Start by developing loving-
kindness towards yourself

Week 14

This week I am thankful for:

_____

_____

_____

_____

_____

_____

_____

_____

_____

_____

_____

_____

_____

_____

_____

2 Minute Mantra Meditation

A mantra is a word or syllable without any particular meaning, that is repeated for the purpose of focusing the mind. It is not an affirmation. You can use any world you like. Some popular mantras are: Om, rama, yam, om namah padme hum. You can use any world you like. Whatever comes to your mind.

Seat yourself in a straight backed chair or sit on the floor with your back straight. Set a timer for 2 minutes.

Breath through your nose and keep your eyes closed. Repeat the mantra you chose in your mind over and over. Think of nothing but your mantra.

Week 15

This week I am thankful for:

_____

_____

_____

_____

_____

_____

_____

_____

_____

_____

_____

_____

_____

_____

_____

_____

_____

2 Minute Third Eye Meditation

Set a timer for 2 minutes.

Sit in your meditation position and focus your attention on the "spot between the eyebrows" (this is sometimes called the "third eye"). If your mind wanders, redirect your thoughts back to this spot.

Week 16

This week I am thankful for:

_____

_____

_____

_____

_____

_____

_____

_____

_____

_____

_____

_____

_____

_____

_____

_____

3 Minute Candle Meditation

Light a tea candle and set it in a safe place. Set a timer for 3 minutes.
Sit in front of the candle and look into the flame. Think only of the flame.
Every time your mind wanders, return back to the flame and continue to look
at it. Over time you will be able to look at the flame without your mind
wandering. It takes time. Start with short intervals

Week 17

This week I am thankful for:

_____

_____

_____

_____

_____

_____

_____

_____

_____

_____

_____

_____

_____

_____

_____

_____

3 Minute Zen Meditation

Seat yourself in a straight backed chair or sit on the floor with your back straight. Set a timer for 3 minutes.

Breath through your nose and keep your eyes lowered, resting your gaze on the ground about two to three feet in front of you.

Concentrate your attention on the movement of your breath going in and out through your nose. Each time you inhale, you count one number, starting with 10, and then moving backward to 9,8 etc. If you get distracted and lose your count, gently bring back the attention to 10 and resume from there.

Week 18

This week I am thankful for:

_____
_____
_____
_____
_____
_____
_____
_____
_____
_____
_____
_____
_____
_____
_____
_____

3 Minute Loving Kindness Meditation

Set a timer for 3 minutes.
Sit in your meditation position, with closed eyes, and generate a feeling of kindness and benevolence in your heart and mind. Start by developing loving-kindness towards yourself.

Week 19

This week I am thankful for:

_____

_____

_____

_____

_____

_____

_____

_____

_____

_____

_____

_____

_____

_____

_____

3 Minute Mantra Meditation

A mantra is a word or syllable without any particular meaning, that is repeated for the purpose of focusing the mind. It is not an affirmation. You can use any world you like. Some popular mantras are: Om, rama, yam, om namah padme hum. You can use any world you like. Whatever comes to your mind.

Seat yourself in a straight backed chair or sit on the floor with your back straight. Set a timer for 3 minutes.

Breath through your nose and keep your eyes closed. Repeat the mantra you chose in your mind over and over. Think of nothing but your mantra.

Week 20

This week I am thankful for:

_____

_____

_____

_____

_____

_____

_____

_____

_____

_____

_____

_____

_____

_____

_____

_____

_____

3 Minute Third Eye Meditation

Set a timer for 3 minutes.
Sit in your meditation position and focus your attention on the "spot between
the eyebrows" (this is sometimes called the "third eye"). If your mind wanders,
redirect your thoughts back to this spot.

Week 21

This week I am thankful for:

_____

_____

_____

_____

_____

_____

_____

_____

_____

_____

_____

_____

_____

_____

_____

_____

3 Minute Candle Meditation

Light a tea candle and set it in a safe place. Set a timer for 3 minutes.
Sit in front of the candle and look into the flame. Think only of the flame. Every time your mind wanders, return back to the flame and continue to look at it. Over time you will be able to look at the flame without your mind wandering. It takes time. Start with short intervals.

Week 22

This week I am thankful for:

_____

_____

_____

_____

_____

_____

_____

_____

_____

_____

_____

_____

_____

_____

_____

3 Minute Zen Meditation

Seat yourself in a straight backed chair or sit on the floor with your back straight. Set a timer for 3 minutes.

Breath through your nose and keep your eyes lowered, resting your gaze on the ground about two to three feet in front of you.

Concentrate your attention on the movement of your breath going in and out through your nose. Each time you inhale, you count one number, starting with 10, and then moving backward to 9,8 etc. If you get distracted and lose your count, gently bring back the attention to 10 and resume from there.

Week 23

This week I am thankful for:

_____
_____
_____
_____
_____
_____
_____
_____
_____
_____
_____
_____
_____
_____
_____
_____
_____

3 Minute Loving Kindness Meditation

Set a timer for 3 minutes.
Sit in your meditation position, with closed eyes, and generate a feeling of kindness and benevolence in your heart and mind. Start by developing loving-kindness towards yourself.

Week 24

This week I am thankful for:

_____

_____

_____

_____

_____

_____

_____

_____

_____

_____

_____

_____

_____

_____

_____

3 Minute Mantra Meditation

A mantra is a word or syllable without any particular meaning, that is repeated for the purpose of focusing the mind. It is not an affirmation. You can use any world you like. Some popular mantras are: Om, rama, yam, om namah padme hum. You can use any world you like. Whatever comes to your mind.

Seat yourself in a straight backed chair or sit on the floor with your back straight. Set a timer for 3 minutes.

Breath through your nose and keep your eyes closed. Repeat the mantra you chose in your mind over and over. Think of nothing but your mantra.

Week 25

This week I am thankful for:

_____

_____

_____

_____

_____

_____

_____

_____

_____

_____

_____

_____

_____

_____

_____

_____

_____

3 Minute Third Eye Meditation

Set a timer for 3 minutes.

Sit in your meditation position and focus your attention on the "spot between the eyebrows" (this is sometimes called the "third eye"). If your mind wanders, redirect your thoughts back to this spot.

Week 26

This week I am thankful for:

_____

_____

_____

_____

_____

_____

_____

_____

_____

_____

_____

_____

_____

_____

_____

3 Minute Candle Meditation

Light a tea candle and set it in a safe place. Set a timer for 3 minutes.
Sit in front of the candle and look into the flame. Think only of the flame. Every time your mind wanders, return back to the flame and continue to look at it. Over time you will be able to look at the flame without your mind wandering. It takes time. Start with short intervals.

Week 27

This week I am thankful for:

_____

_____

_____

_____

_____

_____

_____

_____

_____

_____

_____

_____

_____

_____

3 Minute Zen Meditation

Seat yourself in a straight backed chair or sit on the floor with your back straight. Set a timer for 3 minutes.

Breath through your nose and keep your eyes lowered, resting your gaze on the ground about two to three feet in front of you.

Concentrate your attention on the movement of your breath going in and out through your nose. Each time you inhale, you count one number, starting with 10, and then moving backward to 9,8 etc. If you get distracted and lose your count, gently bring back the attention to 10 and resume from there.

Week 28

This week I am thankful for:

_____

_____

_____

_____

_____

_____

_____

_____

_____

_____

_____

_____

_____

_____

_____

_____

_____

3 Minute Loving Kindness Meditation

Set a timer for 3 minutes.
Sit in your meditation position, with closed eyes, and generate a feeling of kindness and benevolence in your heart and mind. Start by developing loving-kindness towards yourself.

Week 29

This week I am thankful for:

_____

_____

_____

_____

_____

_____

_____

_____

_____

_____

_____

_____

_____

_____

_____

_____

3 Minute Mantra Meditation

A mantra is a word or syllable without any particular meaning, that is repeated for the purpose of focusing the mind. It is not an affirmation. You can use any world you like. Some popular mantras are: Om, rama, yam, om namah padme hum. You can use any world you like. Whatever comes to your mind.

Seat yourself in a straight backed chair or sit on the floor with your back straight. Set a timer for 3 minutes.

Breath through your nose and keep your eyes closed. Repeat the mantra you chose in your mind over and over. Think of nothing but your mantra.

Week 30

This week I am thankful for:

_____
_____
_____
_____
_____
_____
_____
_____
_____
_____
_____
_____
_____
_____
_____
_____
_____

3 Minute Third Eye Meditation

Set a timer for 3 minutes.

Sit in your meditation position and focus your attention on the "spot between the eyebrows" (this is sometimes called the "third eye"). If your mind wanders, redirect your thoughts back to this spot.

Week 31

This week I am thankful for:

_____

_____

_____

_____

_____

_____

_____

_____

_____

_____

_____

_____

_____

_____

_____

_____

3 Minute Candle Meditation

Light a tea candle and set it in a safe place. Set a timer for 3 minutes.
Sit in front of the candle and look into the flame. Think only of the flame.
Every time your mind wanders, return back to the flame and continue to look
at it. Over time you will be able to look at the flame without your mind
wandering. It takes time. Start with short intervals.

Week 32

This week I am thankful for:

_____

_____

_____

_____

_____

_____

_____

_____

_____

_____

_____

_____

_____

_____

_____

3 Minute Zen Meditation

Seat yourself in a straight backed chair or sit on the floor with your back straight. Set a timer for 3 minutes.

Breath through your nose and keep your eyes lowered, resting your gaze on the ground about two to three feet in front of you.

Concentrate your attention on the movement of your breath going in and out through your nose. Each time you inhale, you count one number, starting with 10, and then moving backward to 9,8 etc. If you get distracted and lose your count, gently bring back the attention to 10 and resume from there.

Week 33

This week I am thankful for:

_____
_____

_____
_____
_____
_____
_____
_____
_____
_____
_____
_____
_____
_____
_____
_____

3 Minute Loving Kindness Meditation

Set a timer for 3 minutes.
Sit in your meditation position, with closed eyes, and generate a feeling of kindness and benevolence in your heart and mind. Start by developing loving-kindness towards yourself.

Week 34

This week I am thankful for:

_____

_____

_____

_____

_____

_____

_____

_____

_____

_____

_____

_____

_____

_____

3 Minute Mantra Meditation

A mantra is a word or syllable without any particular meaning, that is repeated for the purpose of focusing the mind. It is not an affirmation. You can use any world you like. Some popular mantras are: Om, rama, yam, om namah padme hum. You can use any world you like. Whatever comes to your mind.

Seat yourself in a straight backed chair or sit on the floor with your back straight. Set a timer for 3 minutes.

Breath through your nose and keep your eyes closed. Repeat the mantra you chose in your mind over and over. Think of nothing but your mantra.

Week 35

This week I am thankful for:

_____
_____
_____
_____
_____
_____
_____
_____
_____
_____
_____
_____
_____
_____
_____

3 Minute Third Eye Meditation

Set a timer for 3 minutes.
Sit in your meditation position and focus your attention on the "spot between
the eyebrows" (this is sometimes called the "third eye"). If your mind wanders,
redirect your thoughts back to this spot.

Week 36

This week I am thankful for:

_____

_____

_____

_____

_____

_____

_____

_____

_____

_____

_____

_____

_____

_____

_____

4 Minute Candle Meditation

Light a tea candle and set it in a safe place. Set a timer for 4 minutes.
Sit in front of the candle and look into the flame. Think only of the flame. Every time your mind wanders, return back to the flame and continue to look at it. Over time you will be able to look at the flame without your mind wandering. It takes time. Start with short intervals.

Week 37

This week I am thankful for:

_____

_____

_____

_____

_____

_____

_____

_____

_____

_____

_____

_____

_____

4 Minute Zen Meditation

Seat yourself in a straight backed chair or sit on the floor with your back straight. Set a timer for 4 minutes.

Breath through your nose and keep your eyes lowered, resting your gaze on the ground about two to three feet in front of you.

Concentrate your attention on the movement of your breath going in and out through your nose. Each time you inhale, you count one number, starting with 10, and then moving backward to 9,8 etc. If you get distracted and lose your count, gently bring back the attention to 10 and resume from there.

Week 38

This week I am thankful for:

_____
_____

_____
_____
_____
_____
_____
_____
_____
_____
_____
_____
_____
_____
_____

4 Minute Loving Kindness Meditation

Set a timer for 4 minutes.
Sit in your meditation position, with closed eyes, and generate a feeling of kindness and benevolence in your heart and mind. Start by developing loving-kindness towards yourself and to the people close to you.

Week 39

This week I am thankful for:

_____

_____

_____

_____

_____

_____

_____

_____

_____

_____

_____

_____

_____

_____

_____

4 Minute Mantra Meditation

A mantra is a word or syllable without any particular meaning, that is repeated for the purpose of focusing the mind. It is not an affirmation. You can use any world you like. Some popular mantras are: Om, rama, yam, om namah padme hum. You can use any world you like. Whatever comes to your mind.

Seat yourself in a straight backed chair or sit on the floor with your back straight. Set a timer for 4 minutes.

Breath through your nose and keep your eyes closed. Repeat the mantra you chose in your mind over and over. Think of nothing but your mantra.

Week 40

This week I am thankful for:

_____

_____

_____

_____

_____

_____

_____

_____

_____

_____

_____

_____

_____

_____

_____

4 Minute Third Eye Meditation

Set a timer for 4 minutes.
Sit in your meditation position and focus your attention on the "spot between
the eyebrows" (this is sometimes called the "third eye"). If your mind wanders,
redirect your thoughts back to this spot.

Week 41

This week I am thankful for:

_____

_____

_____

_____

_____

_____

_____

_____

_____

_____

_____

_____

_____

_____

_____

_____

4 Minute Candle Meditation

Light a tea candle and set it in a safe place. Set a timer for 4 minutes.
Sit in front of the candle and look into the flame. Think only of the flame.
Every time your mind wanders, return back to the flame and continue to look
at it. Over time you will be able to look at the flame without your mind
wandering. It takes time. Start with short intervals.

Week 42

This week I am thankful for:

_____
_____
_____
_____
_____
_____
_____
_____
_____
_____
_____
_____
_____
_____
_____

4 Minute Zen Meditation

Seat yourself in a straight backed chair or sit on the floor with your back straight. Set a timer for 4 minutes.

Breath through your nose and keep your eyes lowered, resting your gaze on the ground about two to three feet in front of you.

Concentrate your attention on the movement of your breath going in and out through your nose. Each time you inhale, you count one number, starting with 10, and then moving backward to 9,8 etc. If you get distracted and lose your count, gently bring back the attention to 10 and resume from there.

Week 43

This week I am thankful for:

_____

_____

_____

_____

_____

_____

_____

_____

_____

_____

_____

_____

_____

_____

_____

_____

4 Minute Loving Kindness meditation

Set a timer for 4 minutes.
Sit in your meditation position, with closed eyes, and generate a feeling of kindness and benevolence in your heart and mind. Start by developing loving-kindness towards yourself and to the people close to you.

Week 44

This week I am thankful for:

_____
_____
_____
_____
_____
_____
_____
_____
_____
_____
_____
_____
_____
_____
_____

4 Minute Mantra Meditation

A mantra is a word or syllable without any particular meaning, that is repeated for the purpose of focusing the mind. It is not an affirmation. You can use any world you like. Some popular mantras are: Om, rama, yam, om namah padme hum. You can use any world you like. Whatever comes to your mind.

Seat yourself in a straight backed chair or sit on the floor with your back straight. Set a timer for 4 minutes.

Breath through your nose and keep your eyes closed. Repeat the mantra you chose in your mind over and over. Think of nothing but your mantra.

Week 45

This week I am thankful for:

_____

_____

_____

_____

_____

_____

_____

_____

_____

_____

_____

_____

_____

_____

_____

_____

3 minute Third Eye Meditation

Set a timer for 3 minutes.
Sit in your meditation position and focus your attention on the "spot between the eyebrows" (this is sometimes called the "third eye"). If your mind wanders, redirect your thoughts back to this spot.

Week 46

This week I am thankful for:

_____

_____

_____

_____

_____

_____

_____

_____

_____

_____

_____

_____

_____

_____

4 Minute Candle Meditation

Light a tea candle and set it in a safe place. Set a timer for 4 minutes.
Sit in front of the candle and look into the flame. Think only of the flame.
Every time your mind wanders, return back to the flame and continue to look
at it. Over time you will be able to look at the flame without your mind
wandering. It takes time. Start with short intervals.

Week 47

This week I am thankful for:

_____
_____
_____
_____
_____
_____
_____
_____
_____
_____
_____
_____
_____
_____

4 Minute Zen Meditation

Seat yourself in a straight backed chair or sit on the floor with your back straight. Set a timer for 4 minutes.

Breath through your nose and keep your eyes lowered, resting your gaze on the ground about two to three feet in front of you.

Concentrate your attention on the movement of your breath going in and out through your nose. Each time you inhale, you count one number, starting with 10, and then moving backward to 9,8 etc. If you get distracted and lose your count, gently bring back the attention to 10 and resume from there.

Week 48

This week I am thankful for:

_____
_____
_____
_____
_____
_____
_____
_____
_____
_____
_____
_____
_____
_____
_____
_____

4 Minute Loving Kindness Meditation

Set a timer for 4 minutes.
Sit in your meditation position, with closed eyes, and generate a feeling of
kindness and benevolence in your heart and mind. Start by developing loving-
kindness towards yourself and to the people close to you.

Week 49

This week I am thankful for:

_____

_____

_____

_____

_____

_____

_____

_____

_____

_____

_____

_____

_____

_____

4 Minute Mantra Meditation

A mantra is a word or syllable without any particular meaning, that is repeated for the purpose of focusing the mind. It is not an affirmation. You can use any world you like. Some popular mantras are: Om, rama, yam, om namah padme hum. You can use any world you like. Whatever comes to your mind.

Seat yourself in a straight backed chair or sit on the floor with your back straight. Set a timer for 4 minutes.

Breath through your nose and keep your eyes closed. Repeat the mantra you chose in your mind over and over. Think of nothing but your mantra.

Week 50

This week I am thankful for:

_____
_____
_____
_____
_____
_____
_____
_____
_____
_____
_____
_____
_____
_____
_____
_____
_____

3 Minute Third Eye Meditation

Set a timer for 3 minutes.
Sit in your meditation position and focus your attention on the "spot between the eyebrows" (this is sometimes called the "third eye"). If your mind wanders, redirect your thoughts back to this spot.

Week 51

This week I am thankful for:

_____

_____

_____

_____

_____

_____

_____

_____

_____

_____

_____

_____

_____

_____

_____

_____

_____

5 Minute Candle Meditation

Light a tea candle and set it in a safe place. Set a timer for 5 minutes.
Sit in front of the candle and look into the flame. Think only of the flame.
Every time your mind wanders, return back to the flame and continue to look
at it. Over time you will be able to look at the flame without your mind
wandering. It takes time. Start with short intervals.

Week 52

This week I am thankful for:

_____

_____

_____

_____

_____

_____

_____

_____

_____

_____

_____

_____

_____

_____

_____

5 Minute Zen Meditation

Seat yourself in a straight backed chair or sit on the floor with your back straight. Set a timer for 5 minutes.

Breath through your nose and keep your eyes lowered, resting your gaze on the ground about two to three feet in front of you.

Concentrate your attention on the movement of your breath going in and out through your nose. Each time you inhale, you count one number, starting with 10, and then moving backward to 9,8 etc. If you get distracted and lose your count, gently bring back the attention to 10 and resume from there.

Made in the USA
Columbia, SC
13 January 2023

10231923R00063